FRANK IS A MIRACLE

Julie Marie Myatt

BROADWAY PLAY PUBLISHING INC
New York
www.broadwayplaypublishing.com
info@broadwayplaypublishing.com

FRANK IS A MIRACLE
© Copyright 2019 Julie Marie Myatt

Cover photo: Julie Marie Myatt

First edition: August 2019
I S B N: 978-0-88145-814-5

Book design: Marie Donovan
Page make-up: Adobe InDesign
Typeface: Palatino

CHARACTERS & SETTING

FRANK, *seventies, German*
HARRIET, *mid-thirties*
AARON, *mid-forties*
DOUGLAS, *early forties*
LEONARD, *a dachshund (German by distant heritage)*

Place: New York

Time: 2013

Suggested music— "Itzhak Perlman plays Fritz Kreisler"

NOTE ON MUSIC

For performance of copyrighted songs, arrangements or recordings referenced in this play, permission of the copyright owner(s) must be obtained. Other songs, arrangements or recordings may be substituted provided permission from the copyright owner(s) of such songs, arrangements or recordings is obtained or songs, arrangements or recordings in the public domain may be substituted.

"Everything can be taken from a man but one thing: the last of the human freedoms—to choose one's attitude in any given set of circumstances, to choose one's way."
Viktor E Frankl

(A city sidewalk)

(Outside an apartment building.)

(Day)

(FRANK stands staring up at a tree. Just staring at a bird)

(HARRIET enters, walking a dachshund.)

(She stops to watch FRANK for a moment. Points to FRANK.)

HARRIET: That man is—
(She quickly points to the dog.)
Oh wait, this is Leonard. If he barks, please ignore him.
That's just what he does. It's a pain in the ass, but it's
who he is. What can I say. He needs to be heard.
(She points to FRANK again.)
That man, is Frank. He lives on my street. He looks
like someone out of an old movie from the forties.
Doesn't he? I mean, look at him. He still wears a hat.
A fedora, no less. He carries an umbrella like its a
cane, even when there is no rain. He is formal in a
way that is both gentle and genteel. He lives alone and
maybe he has family somewhere but I don't know.
I've never seen or heard about them. But then again,
we rarely talk beyond a simple "hello" and "how are
you". Maybe a brief comment about the weather, but
little else. It seems to me, like he has been forgotten by
loved ones. Some days he acts like he has been…well…
just…I have no other way to say it…just, forgotten.
I'm not sure if you've met someone who seems to have
been forgotten, but I think you might know what I
mean if you have. For example. They are often home

in the middle of the day. They are in no hurry to get
anywhere. They take their time at the grocery store—
even when people are trying to rush them in line, they
just keep digging for their money in their pocket to get
the exact change. Or they write a check. They're the last
people, in the world, with a check book, who in public,
will stand there writing a check.
(She takes a moment to look at him, then her dog.)
These forgotten people love all dogs, even the real
barkers. Like this guy.
(She bends down to pet the dog.)
They want to pet them all and tell them they are good.
Even if they're not. Really. Technically. All that. Good.
(To the dog)
Right, Leonard? Good boy.
(She stops petting him.)
They pet cats too. They always stop for small children
and tell them hello. They watch birds in trees.
Incessantly.
(She stops to look at FRANK *again.)*
Almost as if they are afraid they will miss seeing every
bird that passes. Afraid they will miss identifying the
song with the bird. Miss a glimpse of it's wings. Miss
some fleeting beauty.
(Silence)
They stop and sit on benches for hours, just watching
the world go by. And sometimes, some days, they
smell of too much wine or sleep or sadness. Frank does
all these things with a fixed smile on his face, and his
winter coat buttoned up high. I made him a scarf a few
months ago to help keep his neck warm and he cried
when I gave it to him, and walked away. Sometimes,
he disappears, for weeks at a time. I'm not sure where
he goes. Or if he just doesn't come outside. What does
he do with his days? Yesterday, I was standing here
in this very spot, just like this, with Leonard beside

me, thinking all of these things about the life of my neighbor Frank, when he turned to me and said.

(FRANK *turns toward* HARRIET.)

FRANK: Hello Harriet.

HARRIET: Hi Frank.

FRANK: What are you thinking about?

HARRIET: Oh. Nothing particular.

(FRANK *walks over and pets the dog.*)

FRANK: Leonard. How are you, my long friend? You are very good, aren't you? Yes. Yes you are. Good boy.

(*The dog barks.*)

FRANK: Exactly what I was thinking.
(*To* HARRIET)
Why are you home now? It's early, yes—

HARRIET: Personal day.

FRANK: Are you sick?

HARRIET: Depressed.

FRANK: I see. Oh dear.

(HARRIET *pushes a smile.*)

HARRIET: It's not a big deal—

FRANK: What's the problem?

HARRIET: Oh, too much to bore you with.

FRANK: The sunshine helps then, yes?

HARRIET: Yes. Some. Maybe.
(*She sighs.*)
Maybe.
(*She pushes a smile. Again*)
You're still wearing the scarf.

FRANK: Of course.

HARRIET: It's June.

FRANK: Yes.

HARRIET: It's hot out.

FRANK: You made it for me. It's special.

HARRIET: But I don't want you to hurt yourself.

(FRANK smiles.)

HARRIET: Seriously. That wool might give you heat stroke.

FRANK: It's fine.
(He adjust the scarf.)
I like it.

HARRIET: I haven't seen you in awhile. You disappeared.

FRANK: So did you. I noticed.

HARRIET: I was busy.

FRANK: Yes. Me too. Me too.

HARRIET: Doing what?

FRANK: Oh. This and that. You know. Time flies.

HARRIET: Sure.

(FRANK checks his watch.)

FRANK: It's near four o'clock. Well then. Will you come in for tea?

HARRIET: It's five-fifteen, actually.

FRANK: My watch must be broken. Still, we can have tea.

HARRIET: You and me?

FRANK: Yes.

HARRIET: Now?

FRANK: Yes.

HARRIET: Where?

FRANK: In my apartment.

HARRIET: Inside?

FRANK: Yes.
(Long silence)
Are you afraid to come in my apartment?

HARRIET: No. No.

FRANK: I've been meaning to invite you. Since the scarf. To thank you. But…things, you know. Time got away.

HARRIET: Uh. Yes. Great. Okay.

FRANK: Are you sure you're not too busy?
(He smiles.)
With your depression.

HARRIET: No. I'm not *that* depressed. Really. It's just. *(Silence)* A phase.

FRANK: Then you need company. You need people. For this phase.

HARRIET: Maybe.

(HARRIET and FRANK walk to the door in the building.)

FRANK: Just a minute. Let me find my key. Okay.
(He looks for his key. It takes him some time.)
Let's see here.
(He pads every pocket.)
No, not there.

HARRIET: Do you need some help?

FRANK: No. No.
(It is in the last pocket he looks.)
Of course. Yes?
(He holds up the key.)
It's always the last pocket. Why is that?

HARRIET: Life.

FRANK: It keeps you on your toes.
(He finally opens a door.)

(As FRANK *and* HARRIET *enter, the stage becomes* FRANK's *apartment. An apartment that is neatly stacked floor to ceiling with books, newspapers, boxes, furniture, pictures, clothes, artwork, musical instruments, records, and knick knacks paddywacks of every sort.)*

*(*FRANK *is a hoarder. [Neat and organized, and literary, but a hoarder none-the-less.])*

FRANK: As you can see, I'm a bit of a collector.

HARRIET: I see that.
(She picks up the dog [as if he might get buried].)

FRANK: Some things just look too lonesome on the street not to bring inside. Yes?

*(*FRANK *and* HARRIET *wind their way to a table covered in papers that has been set for tea on top of the papers. It's a very nice tea pot and cups and saucers.)*

HARRIET: Were you expecting me?

FRANK: No.

(Silence)

HARRIET: Looks like you're quite the reader.

FRANK: Oh yes.
(He looks at his books with great love.)
Yes. What a world in all those pages. What a world. Everything. Everything.
(Silence)
I used to have a book group on Thursdays but I don't know what happened. People just stopped reading, I guess. Everyone got too old. Or died. I don't know. You have to take care of your eyes. Do you eat carrots?

HARRIET: What?

FRANK: Carrots? Do you eat them?

HARRIET: No. Not really.

FRANK: Please. I beg you. Eat carrots. Every day. I am very serious, Harriet. I eat five carrots a day, and I still have good eyes.

HARRIET: Really?

FRANK: Carrots. Yes. Definitely. They're good for you, and very good for the eyes.

(FRANK *lights the stove. There are papers dangerously close.*)

HARRIET: I'm worried about those papers near the stove.

FRANK: Why?

HARRIET: It looks like they could catch fire.

FRANK: No. They've been there forever. I know what I'm doing. Don't worry.

HARRIET: I worry. It's my nature.

FRANK: Don't. It will make you old. Look at me. I look a hundred. Why? Worry. How old are you? Forty. Forty-six?

(Silence)

HARRIET: Thirty-five.

FRANK: See? You look older because you're unhappy. You worry too much.

HARRIET: I'm not unhappy. What do I have to be unhappy about?

FRANK: You're depressed.

HARRIET: I'm not depressed in a, in a big way—

FRANK: You said so. Just now, outside. You said—

HARRIET: It's an expression. I shouldn't have said anything.

(She tries to smile.)
I can be dramatic. I'm just a little blue.

FRANK: Please. It's on your face, Harriet. You're unhappy. Look at you, dear.

HARRIET: Maybe I should go—

FRANK: Sit down. I'm sorry. I'm sorry. I'm too honest. This is my problem sometimes. Sit.
(Silence)
Are you crying? Oh dear. I'm sorry. I'm sorry.

HARRIET: I just didn't sleep well last night. So.

FRANK: Why not?

HARRIET: I don't know. I had a dream. I couldn't shake it.

FRANK: What was it?

HARRIET: There was a lot of running and screaming and hiding. I don't know.

FRANK: You talk to your husband? Did he comfort you?

HARRIET: I don't have a husband.

FRANK: I thought you had a husband.

HARRIET: No.

FRANK: Did you once? Before? There was a man with you. He lived with you?

HARRIET: We weren't married.

FRANK: No?

HARRIET: No.

FRANK: That's too bad. What was his name?

HARRIET: Seth.

FRANK: Seth. Yes. Yes. Nice man. I liked him.

HARRIET: Me too.

FRANK: I remember he was funny.

(Silence)

HARRIET: Yes. Very.

FRANK: What happened?
(Silence)
Are you crying again?

HARRIET: No.

FRANK: Please.

(FRANK hands HARRIET a napkin.)

HARRIET: Thank you.

FRANK: I'm sorry.

HARRIET: No, I'm sorry. I'm just…I don't know.

FRANK: So this is why you are depressed and blue?

(HARRIET nods.)

FRANK: Things will get better. You have to think positive.

(HARRIET wipes her eyes.)

FRANK: I'll put on some music. That will help.
(He walks over to his music collection.)

HARRIET: What about your family?

FRANK: What about them?

HARRIET: Are they—

FRANK: You are depressed. Let's talk about something else—

HARRIET: It's an expression. I told you, I'm fine. Really. I'm sure it's all for the best.
(Silence)
It'll pass. Eventually.
(She smiles.)

(FRANK *places a record on a record player. Itzak Perlman plays Fritz Kreisler,* Slavonic Dance No. 3 in G Major.)

FRANK: It usually does. From my experience. It's good you can cry. And, it's good you have a dog.
(*He listens to the music for a moment.*)
Yes, that is nice. You like it?

HARRIET: Very nice.

FRANK: Itzak Perlman. He is very talented.
(*He dances a few steps with the music.*)
This will help your spirit.
(*A few more dance moves*)

HARRIET: Frank—

FRANK: Let us listen for a moment. No, let us dance.

(FRANK *takes* HARRIET's *hand.*)

HARRIET: Frank, I—

FRANK: Please.

(FRANK *and* HARRIET *dance to the music.*)

FRANK: Good for the spirit, yes?

HARRIET: Yes.

FRANK: Of course.

(*The kettle whistles.*)

FRANK: Oh dear.
(*He walks over and pours hot water into a tea pot.*)
However, I will tell you, Harriet, I once went two years, and this feeling, did not pass. I kept waiting and waiting. I read books. I took walks. I listened to music. So much music, my dreams had their own orchestra. My psyche was in an opera every night. I woke, exhausted. I drank tonics. I ate vegetables. And psht. Nothing. I could not shake it. So, finally, I said okay,

okay, it will not go away, so I will make friends with this feeling. I will call it Steve.

HARRIET: Steve?

FRANK: Yes.

HARRIET: Why Steve?

FRANK: I thought, okay, maybe this is an American feeling. I will give it an American name. Steve. We will be friends and talk to each other, and laugh maybe. And eventually, one day, when I wasn't looking, I tell you this honestly, Steve walked out the door and the feeling was gone too. He did not say good-bye, he just left. Like that.

HARRIET: Did you miss him?

FRANK: No. Steve could be unpleasant.

HARRIET: What started it?

FRANK: The feeling?

HARRIET: Yes.

FRANK: My second wife died.

HARRIET: Well, of course. That's to be expected.

FRANK: Yes. Yes. Of course. But I can't say why Steve had to stay so long. Why so long? I had other pains, in my life. My wife and I didn't have a happy marriage. We were good enough companions, but we fought. Often. Very often.

HARRIET: Why?

FRANK: Why what?

HARRIET: Why'd you fight?

FRANK: Who knows really. I was not enough for her. She wanted more out of life then she thought I had to offer her. Maybe. I don't know anymore.

HARRIET: What do you do for a living?

FRANK: I was a doctor.

HARRIET: That wasn't enough for her?

FRANK: She wanted a lawyer.

(He shrugs.)

She liked men who talked fast. Confident. Loud. She would have liked Steve. They would have been happy together.

HARRIET: Where'd you meet?

FRANK: I don't want to talk about me.

HARRIET: I'm curious—

FRANK: It's a beautiful day. You are unhappy. Why push it?

HARRIET: Actually, Frank, I would find it a great relief to think about someone else beside myself right now.

FRANK: That, my dear, is a great relief to us all.

HARRIET: Maybe.

FRANK: That is the secret. Forget yourself. Forget yourself all together.

(Silence)

(FRANK and HARRIET drink tea.)

FRANK: Yes, I think that is the secret.

(Silence)

HARRIET: You're German?

FRANK: Yes.

HARRIET: I thought so.

FRANK: Like your dog.

(Silence)

HARRIET: Do you have children?

FRANK: There you go.

HARRIET: What?

FRANK: Asking about me again. Looking for more relief?

HARRIET: Yes.

(Silence)

FRANK: I have two children. Yes.

HARRIET: Do they live in New York?

FRANK: How's your tea?

(HARRIET tastes it.)

HARRIET: Oh. Good. Thank you.

FRANK: It's from India, this tea.

HARRIET: Really?

FRANK: Have you been there?

HARRIET: India? Yes. Years ago.

FRANK: Really? Traveling?

HARRIET: When I was in college. I went with a boyfriend.

FRANK: Seth?

HARRIET: No. Another one. He was into Yoga. And gurus. So.

FRANK: I see.

HARRIET: Yes.

FRANK: Wonderful place, India I went once. I smelled things there that make New York look like a rose garden. But, I've smelled worse, I guess—

AARON: *(O S)* Dad? Are you back?

(A man in a wheelchair wheels in from a back bed room. He's in his forties. Beard. He wears glasses that are broken in the middle. This is AARON.)

AARON: Is it time for tea? I need some caffeine. Now.
And I'm starving—

FRANK: Yes, Aaron. Come.

AARON: I was waiting for you, and—
(He stops when he sees HARRIET.*)*
Who's this?

FRANK: Harriet.

*(*AARON *looks* HARRIET *over. Rather seductively)*

FRANK: She is—

AARON: The girl who made you the scarf.

FRANK: The woman who made the scarf for me.Yes.

AARON: That's what I meant. Woman.

FRANK: Harriet, this is my son, Aaron.

AARON: Why are you staring at me?

HARRIET: Was I? I'm sorry. I'm just—

AARON: Is it the wheelchair?

HARRIET: No.

AARON: My glasses? My dad is supposed to get them
fixed—

HARRIET: Neither. None. No. No. I just didn't know
anyone else lived here—

AARON: Well, now you know.
(He rolls up to the table.)

AARON: You know he won't take that scarf off.

HARRIET: I see that.

FRANK: I like it.

AARON: He's crazy. Your dog bite?

HARRIET: He barks.

FRANK: It is worse than his bite.

AARON: I'll keep my distance. He's pretty short, isn't he?

HARRIET: Yes.

FRANK: That dog is called a dachshund.

AARON: I know what it's called. They were bred to hunt badgers.

FRANK: Dachs means badger. In German. Hund means dog—

AARON: I know! She knows! Jesus. Everyone knows. You don't have to teach every second of the goddamn day.

(Silence)

FRANK: I wasn't teaching.

AARON: Badgers are mean as hell. Your dog must be brave.

HARRIET: No. Not really.

AARON: He's cute. He's got that going for him.

HARRIET: Yes.

AARON: Cute can go a long way. In my book.

FRANK: You could have changed your shirt, Aaron.

AARON: I didn't know we had company. I had my headphones on.

FRANK: Those are going to ruin your ears.

AARON: Then I'll go deaf happy.
(To HARRIET*)*
You into music?

HARRIET: Pardon?

AARON: Are you in to *music*? *Music.*

HARRIET: Oh. Yes. Sure. I like music.

AARON: What kind?

HARRIET: Oh, all kinds, really.

AARON: Specifically…?

HARRIET: Well, uh—

AARON: This stuff? Classical?

HARRIET: Yes. Sure.

AARON: Dad likes classical. Obviously.

FRANK: It is the only music I enjoy.

AARON: He's limited.

FRANK: I know what is beautiful. What is special. That music is meant to take a mind to so many places—

AARON: What about the heart? The heart, Dad. It's more important than the mind.

FRANK: I don't know about that—

AARON: I know.

FRANK: They are both important.

AARON: I try and tell him that there are lots of other kinds. Of music. Folk. Rock and Roll. Jazz. Blue grass. Led Zeppelin has it's charms—

FRANK: More tea, Harriet.

HARRIET: I'm fine. Thank you.

FRANK: Aaron will talk forever on this subject.

AARON: What, you have somewhere to be?

(FRANK *refills* HARRIET'*s cup.*)

AARON: She said "no" on the tea.

HARRIET: That's, that's fine.

AARON: He doesn't listen.

HARRIET: How long have you lived here, Aaron?

AARON: Four months and three days.

HARRIET: I'm surprised I haven't seen you—

AARON: I don't go outside.

(Silence)

FRANK: Aaron used to live up north. What was the name of the town again?

AARON: Plattsburgh.

HARRIET: That's up there.

AARON: I've lived a lot of places.

HARRIET: Oh really? Where?

AARON: Where? Texas, Georgia, Alaska, Kentucky—

FRANK: This is his home now.

AARON: Mississippi. Memphis. Rhode Island. San Francisco—

FRANK: Okay. We don't need the entire list.

AARON: She asked.

FRANK: The sun will rise and set again before you are finished.

AARON: I'm a man on the go. What can I say.
(Silence)
Was.

HARRIET: Well. Aaron. Welcome.

AARON: I am living proof, that no matter how far you go—and I went far, trust me, far as I could go—you can't escape family.

FRANK: I am happy to have you.

AARON: It's a little cramped for two people. My father doesn't believe in throwing anything away. Clearly. Look at this stuff.

HARRIET: He's got an interesting mix of—

AARON: I, on the other hand, am happy with just the clothes on my back. A simple life. Unburdened.

FRANK: More tea, Aaron?

AARON: Let me ask you something. What's your name again?
(He snaps his fingers to remember.)
I took a blow to the head recently, so occasionally I forget things—

FRANK: Her name is Harriet. More tea?

AARON: I asked *her*, Dad. Not you. But yes. More tea. Thank you.
(To HARRIET*)*
Your name?

HARRIET: Harriet.

AARON: Otherwise, my memory is perfect. You're a bit young for that name. Harriet sounds like a woman pushing eighty. What do you do for a living?

HARRIET: I design clothes.

AARON: What?

HARRIET: I design clothing.

AARON: For a living?

HARRIET: Yes—

AARON: You make a real living, designing clothes, for other people?

HARRIET: Yes.

AARON: Seriously?

HARRIET: Seriously.

FRANK: She's talented. Look at this scarf.

AARON: How can you make a living doing that?

HARRIET: I make a pattern, and I—

AARON: And people buy it?

FRANK: She's talented. She has skill. Aaron, please.

AARON: I want to make a living with music. Designing music. For movies. Do you think I could do that?

FRANK: I told you, you have no skill yet. You have to take a class first. Go back to school—

AARON: I didn't ask you!

FRANK: I said you can learn—

AARON: Harriet?

HARRIET: I, I don't know.

AARON: I can't work like I used to. I did construction. As you can see, by the wheels, things have recently taken a turn for the worse.

FRANK: They will get better.

AARON: No they won't.

FRANK: It's all about attitude. Your *will*. You can—

AARON: *Don't. Frank.*

(Silence)

AARON: Motorcycle accident.

HARRIET: Oh.

AARON: Yeah. Sucked. Big time. I was a mess. They pretty much had to stitch me back together.

FRANK: I'm sure Harriet doesn't want to hear the details.

AARON: How do you know?

FRANK: She's depressed already.

HARRIET: I'm not really so depress—

AARON: What are you depressed about?

FRANK: It's none of our business.

AARON: Why not? What else do we have to think about? Look at us. Do we have schedules here?

FRANK: There is plenty for us to do, and think about—

AARON: *(To* HARRIET*)* What's the problem?

HARRIET: It's just, it's just a strange time. In my life.

AARON: How?

HARRIET: It's just is.

AARON: How?

FRANK: She doesn't want—

AARON: I am talking to her, not you!

(Silence)

HARRIET: Things have just worked out differently than I imagined.

AARON: Well, you are preaching to the choir on that one. Try getting used to having no legs. You smoke?

HARRIET: Cigarettes? No—

AARON: Weed. It helps.

FRANK: Of course she doesn't.

HARRIET: Sometimes.

AARON: You want some?

HARRIET: Now? Oh no. No thank you—

AARON: I have a prescription. It's legal.

FRANK: This is tea time, not, not Woodstock, Aaron. Please.

AARON: You don't even know what Woodstock is.

FRANK: Yes I do.

AARON: *(To* HARRIET*)* The weed helps. I'd be happy to get you some—

FRANK: I don't like it.

HARRIET: I'm fine—

AARON: Are you the one living with the pain, Dad?
Huh?

(Silence)

Can you understand that I have pain too?

FRANK: Please, son. Not now—

AARON: C'mon, Dad. She smokes weed. She's pretty.
Who do I have to talk to around here? Who is my age?
And attractive? I thought that's why you invited her—

HARRIET: Actually, I'm probably younger than you—

AARON: How old are you, forty-five, forty-six?

HARRIET: Thirty-five.

AARON: So you're mature for your age. Big deal.

FRANK: She's just unhappy.

AARON: You're beautiful. What does it matter what age
you are?

(Silence)

HARRIET: It matters.

FRANK: You're making her uncomfortable.

AARON: How?

FRANK: This is why you did not marry. You have no
charm with women, Aaron. You are like, like a bull in a
china shop.

AARON: Really? Do I look like a bull?
(He grabs the wheels of his wheelchair)
Is this any kind of symbol of masculinity? Metal?
Wheels? Impotence?

FRANK: I'm speaking metaphorically—

AARON: Duh. Jesus, Dad—

FRANK: I just wish you could be more—

AARON: More what? More like you? Of course you do—

FRANK: No. I didn't say that—

AARON: More like Daniel? Please. As if he knew a thing about women. Or anyone. He is the most selfish man on earth.

FRANK: I am not talking about Daniel. You have such potential.

AARON: Okay. Okay. Let's don't go down that road, mister.

(Silence)

*(*HARRIET *checks her watch.)*

HARRIET: I should probably go.

AARON & FRANK: No.

FRANK: No.

AARON: Why?

FRANK: So soon?

HARRIET: It's getting late and Leonard hasn't eaten his dinner—

FRANK: I should have offered you both food. What was I thinking. Are you hungry? I have so many distractions lately, I forgot to offer you—

HARRIET: No, no—

FRANK: Of course if you are depressed, you are not eating enough. Let me make you something to eat.

AARON: She's not hungry, Dad.

FRANK: Of course she is. It's time for dinner. She has to eat.

AARON: Then let's order food.

FRANK: I can cook.

AARON: No. Let's order from the deli.

FRANK: But—

AARON: I'll pay.

FRANK: You are wasting your money.

AARON: It's my money. To waste. Harriet, what do you want?

HARRIET: Oh, nothing for me.

AARON: I'm buying us dinner, right now, so don't argue with the cripple. What do you want?

HARRIET: Oh—

AARON: Dad, do we have any wine? We'll make it a party.

FRANK: No. I'm sorry. We don't have any wine—

AARON: Why not?

FRANK: You drank it.

AARON: All of it?

FRANK: Yes.

AARON: What do you want to eat, Harriet?

HARRIET: I'm really not hungry—

FRANK: You have to eat. You can't walk around hungry. It's not good for you. Let me cook.

AARON: I want to order in.

FRANK: No, let me cook. It will be—

AARON: I need the outside world, Okay! I need to *taste* the outside world! Please! Just let me get a small piece of it. In my fucking mouth!
(Silence)
It's not much to ask.

FRANK: Okay. Okay.
(Silence)

I understand.

(*Silence*)

AARON: What do you want?

(*Silence*)

FRANK: I want a pastrami sandwich on rye bread.
Please.

AARON: Mustard?

FRANK: Please.

AARON: Harriet?

(*Silence*)

HARRIET: I'll, I'll just get a salad of some sort.

AARON: You can't just get a salad.

FRANK: That's not enough.

AARON: Get tuna fish or something. Protein.

FRANK: And I'll give the dog some of my sandwich. For
his dinner. It is too big for me.

AARON: What's it going to be? Tuna? Chicken salad.

HARRIET: Okay. A side, a side of tuna salad.

AARON: With the salad?

HARRIET: Yes. Please. Thank you.

(AARON *looks* HARRIET *over.*)

AARON: What are you afraid of? Getting fat? Look at
you—

HARRIET: No, I just—

AARON: Seriously. You're perfect. Now look at me.
All hell has broken loose over here. I'm going to eat a
reuben and fries and I don't care.
(*He pats his stomach.*)
I'm drowning my sorrows in food.

HARRIET: I just don't eat much.

AARON: I can tell. Dad, do you want fries?

FRANK: No. No.

AARON: I'm getting fries for you. You know you want them. Where's the phone? Let's order from that deli down the street you like. What's it called—

FRANK: Arty's? No. That's gotten too expensive—

AARON: You said you like that place.

FRANK: It doesn't matter—

AARON: That's the one I want. Give me the phone.

(FRANK *finds the phone. He hands it to* AARON.)

FRANK: Don't order drinks. We can—

AARON: I'm getting a coke. Harriet?

HARRIET: I'm fine—

AARON: Come on.

HARRIET: Really. No, thank you.

FRANK: She doesn't want it.

AARON: What's the number?

FRANK: 212-555-9876.

(AARON *dials.*)

AARON: This phone smells like chicken.

FRANK: That's impossible.

AARON: Have you smelled it?
(*Into phone*)
Hi. Yeah, I want to place an order for delivery. Yes. Dad, what's your address?

FRANK: Tell them Frank's apartment.

AARON: They know your apartment?

FRANK: Yes.

AARON: How?

FRANK: They just do, Aaron.

AARON: *(Into phone)* Frank's apartment… That Frank, yes… No, I'm his son… He has a son, yes…. How long? Since 1968. Jesus…yes… What is this, twenty questions? Can I order already? Yeah…give me a pastrami on rye—

FRANK: With mustard—

AARON: I was going to say mustard—
(Into phone)
With mustard, a reuben, a salad…you know, a regular salad, with lettuce—
(To HARRIET*)*
What kind of dressing?

HARRIET: Oil and vinegar.

*(*AARON *looks at* HARRIET.*)*

AARON: Jesus Christ.

HARRIET: What?

AARON: Live a little, will you?

HARRIET: I like it.

AARON: Do you like blue cheese?

HARRIET: It's okay—

AARON: *(Into phone)* Blue cheese. And oil and vinegar… both, on the side…that's fine… And a side of tuna salad… Two orders of fries. And three cokes.

FRANK: I don't want—

AARON: Yes you do.
(Into phone)
Yeah. I'm going to put it on my credit card.

FRANK: Credit? No, no. I'll get my check book—

(AARON *puts his hand up to stop* FRANK, *continues in the phone.*)

AARON: Uh huh.

(He takes out his wallet.)

Give me a minute.

FRANK: *(To* HARRIET, *quietly)* (I'm sorry for my son.)

AARON: What'd you say, Dad.

FRANK: Nothing, Aaron.

AARON: *(Into phone)* Are you ready? I'm ready. I'm ready. Jesus. It's a Visa. 479200037846....7846...6...uh huh... How long? Okay. Yeah. Thanks. Uh huh.

HARRIET: (Oh. No, Frank. He's fine.)

FRANK: (I'm afraid, at times, he is a lot like Steve.)

(AARON *hangs up the phone.*)

AARON: Twenty minutes.

FRANK: That's fast.

AARON: They better not fuck it up.

FRANK: They won't. I know the owner. His prices are too expensive now, but he is very competent—

AARON: Please don't whisper about me. I hate that.

FRANK: I was not whispering about you—

AARON: Do you watch T V, Harriet?

HARRIET: Uh. Yes. Some. Yes.

AARON: My dad hates T V. He doesn't own one anymore. It's torture here.

FRANK: Look at all these books? And music. Why do I need television?

AARON: Entertainment. I don't know what you have against *entertainment*. I need some—

FRANK: That's not entertainment.

AARON: Yes it is.

FRANK: Not for me. I'm happy without it.

HARRIET: You can watch T V on your computer. Do you have a computer?

AARON: It's not the same. Sitting in front of the screen alone. My whole life is solitary now.

HARRIET: I guess—

AARON: I'm a fucking shut-in.
(He laughs.)
Hell. Do you know what that's like?

HARRIET: I can imagine.

AARON: You're a bit of a loner, aren't you.

FRANK: You must keep a positive attitude, Aaron. You must. It's very important. You have to think—

AARON: I have to be honest.

FRANK: Yes, okay, but you can't be cynical. I won't have a cynic in my house.

AARON: You'd rather have a liar?

FRANK: I want someone who tries. You must *try. Try.*

AARON: You survive the Holocaust and you are the fucking expert on everything.

(Silence)

FRANK: I've never said that.

AARON: You never have to. Did you know that about my father, Harriet?

HARRIET: Know what?

AARON: What he's been through? In his life?

HARRIET: No.

AARON: Really?

FRANK: Please, son—

AARON: You wouldn't believe it. It's something straight out of a novel. If it wasn't true, you wouldn't believe it. Honest.

FRANK: Aaron, I am asking you—

AARON: My father, your scarf-wearing friend, Frank Gromke—

FRANK: Aaron—

AARON: Is a miracle. In the flesh.

FRANK: Stop it.

AARON: I'm serious, Dad.

FRANK: Harriet is our guest. She doesn't want to listen to this.

AARON: Why not?

FRANK: She's depressed.

HARRIET: I'm, I'm really not *that* depressed. I should have never said anything—

AARON: Well, if she hears your story, she'll feel like a million bucks. I'll tell you that much. She'll count her chickens. I mean her blessings. Count her blessings. I know I do. I count my blessings everyday.

FRANK: Aaron—

AARON: I have counted my chickens too, but that's never a good idea. That's a big mistake.

FRANK: You are being sarcastic.

AARON: I'm not! Are, or are you not, a living, breathing—

FRANK: I am human being, like any other.

AARON: Bullshit! And you know it!

FRANK: Harriet. I'm sorry.

AARON: Don't use humility like that. Please. It's so fucking irritating—

FRANK: I'm not—

AARON: Harriet. Let me tell you something. About my father.

Do you have a moment?

(HARRIET *just looks at* AARON.)

HARRIET: Uh—

AARON: My father, this *humble* man right here, escaped from a concentration camp in Germany at six years old. Six! His entire family was gassed—

FRANK: Aaron—

AARON: He found a way out, through a toilet. A toilet! A fucking shit-filled toilet and he walked all the way to Switzerland. Switzerland! Can you imagine? Do you know how far that is?
(Silence)
Do you?

HARRIET: Oh. I'm sorry. You're asking me? I thought it was a rhetorical—

FRANK: It wasn't a toilet.

AARON: Sewer. Whatever. And it was far. Switzerland. Thousands of miles. He almost starved to death along the way. Six years old, all by himself. And you know what he did when he got there? He became a doctor. A doctor!

FRANK: I wasn't by myself.

AARON: I'm giving her the abridged version. Obviously. He got some help along the way—

FRANK: Stop it.

AARON: He worked so hard, he studied like a maniac, worked to pay his way, and he became a doctor. He met a young woman—

FRANK: Stop.

AARON: They got married. A simple wedding. They quickly had two daughters together. Beautiful girls. And you know what?

FRANK: Aaron.

AARON: She killed herself, and their two baby girls. With a gas oven. Of all things.

FRANK: No—

AARON: She too, was in the camps, but, she did not have the same strength of spirit as my father. The same moxie. His ability to cling to hope. Hope beyond all hope. And this guy here knows how to cling. Look around you.

FRANK: Please.

AARON: She, this young bride, did not even *try*.

FRANK: Stop.

AARON: And then, then, undeterred from yet another tragedy, another life set-back, he reached for a new horizon. Hope leading the way. He got a fellowship at a hospital here in New York. A new land. A new start. Brave, he crossed the ocean with his broken heart in his hand, and lo and behold, two months later, he meets my—

(The doorbell buzzes O S.)

AARON: Ah. Dinner's here. That was fast. Hold that thought. I'll get it.
(He wheels over to the intercom.)

FRANK: (Harriet.)

AARON: Don't talk behind my back, Dad.

FRANK: (My son is…he is—)

HARRIET: (It's alright. Really. Frank—)

FRANK: (Since the accident. He's very…angry. We hadn't seen each other in many years, and now…)

AARON: *(Into intercom)* Is this the deli or a thief?

VOICE *(O S, chipper, laughing)* Lucky you, it's the deli!

AARON: Come up then.

VOICE *(O S, chipper)* Will do!

(AARON wheels back over. He turns off the music.)

FRANK: Please ask before you turn off my music, Aaron. I have told you this many times already—

AARON: The violin was grinding on my nerves—

FRANK: That is Itzak Perlman —

AARON: I don't care—

FRANK: Well, I'm sorry, but—

AARON: We need to clear some space to eat. I don't know how the hell you live like this.

FRANK: Don't start. Please. Please, son.

AARON: I'm serious. We could get buried under all this shit and no one would find us.

FRANK: I'd be happy to be buried by my books.

AARON: Of course you would. And it's cheaper than a cemetery. It's a win win.

(A knock on the door of the apartment.)

VOICE *(O S, chipper)* It's still not a thief!

FRANK: Aaron. I am telling you.

AARON: What are you telling me?

HARRIET: I'll get the door.

FRANK: Thank you, dear.

(To AARON*)*
Enough.

AARON: C'mon.

FRANK: I mean it. Please, son.

AARON: Relax.

FRANK: What do you want me to say? What?

AARON: Nothing.

FRANK: Are you trying to embarrass me?

AARON: No.

FRANK: Humiliate me in front of our guest? Why?

AARON: No. God. Relax.

FRANK: I wanted to make you happy. I thought it might make you happy. To have some company.

AARON: Really?

FRANK: She is a kind person. What do you want? I don't understand.

*(*HARRIET *opens the door to* DOUGLAS*. Early-forties. He wears a bow-tie.)*

DOUGLAS: Hey. I know you.

HARRIET: You do?

DOUGLAS: You're Harriet.

HARRIET: Yes…
(Silence)
I don't know your name. Sorry—

DOUGLAS: Usually I'm handing you a cup of coffee. Milk. No sugar.

HARRIET: Uh—

DOUGLAS: Douglas.

HARRIET: Douglas. Right. Right. Of course.

DOUGLAS: I've never told you my name before.

HARRIET: I didn't think so—

DOUGLAS: Funny meeting you here.

HARRIET: Yeah. I'm visiting Frank. And his, uh—

DOUGLAS: Where's your dog?

HARRIET: He's sitting over there. Somewhere.

DOUGLAS: He really goes with you everywhere, doesn't he.

AARON: Is this your boyfriend, Harriet?

HARRIET: He works at the deli.

AARON: Yeah. I gathered that.

(DOUGLAS *walks over and puts out his hand.*)

DOUGLAS: Douglas.

AARON: Nice tie.

DOUGLAS: Oh. Thank you. I have a collection.
(*He keeps out his hand.*)
I think I have about forty or so.

AARON: Really?

DOUGLAS: I've lost count.

(AARON *finally meets* DOUGLAS' *handshake.*)

AARON: Douglas. So very formal. Aaron.

DOUGLAS: You're Frank's son?

AARON: That I am.

DOUGLAS: Wow. My dad told me you called. I couldn't believe it. We didn't know Frank had a son.

AARON: He has two.

DOUGLAS: Wow. You don't say.

(*Silence*)

AARON: I say.

DOUGLAS: Wow.

AARON: It's not that exciting. Ask my dad.

DOUGLAS: You keeping your kids a secret, Frank?

FRANK: No.

AARON: He has a lot of secrets. But we aren't one of them.
(*He takes the food.*)
Let me give you a tip.

FRANK: I'll get the tip.

AARON: I've got it, Dad.

FRANK: Let me.

AARON: No! I've got it! Just let me do it. I'm not a fucking child.
(*Silence*)
I have money.

FRANK: Fine.

HARRIET: You want to sit down for a minute, Douglas?

DOUGLAS: I really should get back to work. My dad is waiting—

HARRIET: Aaron just moved here. He doesn't know many people in the neighborhood.

DOUGLAS: Really?

AARON: Really.

DOUGLAS: Well, heck, I'd be more than happy to introduce you to some people. What's your thing?

AARON: My "thing"?

DOUGLAS: What do you like to do?

AARON: Sulk. Mostly.

DOUGLAS: Huh.

AARON: Or smoke weed.

DOUGLAS: I see.

FRANK: Aaron.

AARON: Am I wrong?

(Silence)

FRANK: No. That's quite accurate.

AARON: OK then.

FRANK: It's pathetic.

AARON: Of course it is. Mr. Superman. Of course it is. I am weak and pathetic.

FRANK: I didn't say that. Let's eat. We're all hungry.

DOUGLAS: Well, I don't think I know any sulkers, per say, but I know a lot of people who smoke weed. You'd have something in common with them.

HARRIET: Great.

(AARON just looks at HARRIET.)

HARRIET: Aren't you in a band? I've seen your flyers—

DOUGLAS: Indeed.

HARRIET: Aaron's really interested in music.

DOUGLAS: Wow.
(Silence)
That's great.

AARON: You're very enthusiastic, aren't you.

(Silence)

DOUGLAS: I guess I am.
(He smiles. Laughing)
Is that a crime?

FRANK: No.

AARON: It's just weird.
(Silence)

You're Jewish?

DOUGLAS: One hundred percent.

AARON: Unbelievable.

FRANK: I find it refreshing.

AARON: Of course you do.

DOUGLAS: What kind, what kind of music do you like, Aaron?

AARON: You name it, I like it. If it's good. If it's true. Authentic.

DOUGLAS: Sure, sure.

AARON: Music you probably don't like.

DOUGLAS: Like what?

AARON: The Grateful Dead. For starters.

DOUGLAS: I love the Dead. C'mon.
(He beams.)
They're one of my favorite bands. Their awesome.

(AARON just looks at DOUGLAS.)

DOUGLAS: Don't you think?
(Silence)
You clearly have good taste.
(He smiles.)
Like me.

AARON: We have nothing in common.

DOUGLAS: We have the Dead.
(He smiles.)
That's cool.

(Silence)

AARON: What's your band play?

DOUGLAS: What do you mean?

AARON: What kind of *music* does your band—

DOUGLAS: Oh. Blue Grass.

AARON: Blue Grass?

DOUGLAS: Yep.

AARON: And you're from New York?

DOUGLAS: Yeah.

AARON: Really?

DOUGLAS: Yep.

AARON: How can you play Blue Grass?

DOUGLAS: We just…play it.

AARON: How?

(*Silence*)

DOUGLAS: With instruments. And good spirit.

AARON: Have you ever been to the south?

DOUGLAS: No.

AARON: The mountains?

DOUGLAS: No.

AARON: Appalachia?

DOUGLAS: No.

AARON: Have you ever eaten a biscuit?

(DOUGLAS *thinks*.)

DOUGLAS: No.

AARON: Ever had corn bread? Tasted moonshine?

DOUGLAS: No, but—

AARON: Then how the hell can you play Blue Grass—

DOUGLAS: Not yet. I haven't done those things yet. I
mean—

AARON: It can't be authentic then. The music.

DOUGLAS: Why?

AARON: It just can't.

FRANK: You don't know that, son.

AARON: I know.

DOUGLAS: Well, the Grateful Dead played Blue Grass, and, and—

AARON: They're special.

DOUGLAS: But—

AARON: Don't compare yourself to them. Please. I may vomit.

FRANK: Aaron—

DOUGLAS: I'm not comparing myself to—

AARON: You don't know what Blue Grass is, if you have never seen it's roots. Tasted the country. Eaten a plate of grits. Fatback. Smelled coal dust. Seen poverty. Etc. So…please. Please don't talk to me about your phony Blue Grass music. Hand me my sandwich.

FRANK: He could have studied this music in school. He could have learned from a mentor. There are other ways.

AARON: No. You have to go to the source. Hand me that sandwich. Please.

FRANK: He could learn it from other musicians, Aaron. There are other ways to learn things. Many ways. When you have talent, and discipline, you will find a way.
(He passes out the food.)
Remember that.
(To DOUGLAS*)*
Where did you study music, Douglas?
(Silence)

DOUGLAS: Juilliard.

AARON: (Of course.)

(He laughs.)

Of course!

FRANK: Juilliard. Wonderful.

(To AARON*)*

See, you can do anything you put your mind to.
Juilliard is a very prestigious place.

AARON: Yeah, I've heard of it.

FRANK: He must be very good at this Blue Grass.

*(*HARRIET *smiles at* DOUGLAS.*)*

AARON: My dad thinks he is the expert on everything.

FRANK: That's not true.

(Silence)

DOUGLAS: I did have some very good teachers.

AARON: Frank doesn't even know what Blue Grass is.

FRANK: I do too.

(Silence)

I watched that, that, what do you call it…*Hee Haw.* I
watched *Hee Haw* with you, Aaron. When you were a
boy.

*(*AARON *just shakes his head.)*

FRANK: You liked that show very much.

(Long silence)

DOUGLAS: Lovely weather we had today.

HARRIET: Yes.

DOUGLAS: Sunshine. Just perfect.

HARRIET: Very nice.

(Silence)

DOUGLAS: It looks like you collect instruments, Frank.

FRANK: Pardon me?

DOUGLAS: Musical instruments.

(He smiles.)

You sure have a lot of them. Wow.

AARON: He collects everything. It's pathological.

FRANK: It is not.

AARON: What is it then?

FRANK: Passion.

AARON: Half this stuff you found on the street.

FRANK: So? It was still good. Discarded for no good reason. People waste too much. I clean it up, and it is good as new.

AARON: People want to let go of things. Free themselves. You could learn something.

FRANK: Eat your sandwich.

AARON: Give me nothing but the clothes on my back. That's freedom.

FRANK: Or poverty.

AARON: True. I'll give you that one, Dad. I have known poverty. I could play Blue Grass.

HARRIET: I've heard your band is good, Douglas.

DOUGLAS: You have?

HARRIET: Yeah.

DOUGLAS: Wow. Really?

HARRIET: Uh huh.

DOUGLAS: From who?

HARRIET: My neighbor Gina. She saw one of your shows once.

DOUGLAS: Really? Gina with the blond hair? Cream two sugars?

HARRIET: Yes.

DOUGLAS: She came to my show?

HARRIET: Uh huh.

DOUGLAS: Why didn't you come?

HARRIET: Uh, well. I've been busy. Lately. And—

DOUGLAS: I'm just giving you a hard time—

HARRIET: Oh.

DOUGLAS: But I'll put you and Seth on the list next time. You can come for free—

AARON: You play the banjo?

DOUGLAS: I'm sorry?

AARON: You play the banjo, Mr Bluegrass.

DOUGLAS: I do.

AARON: Seriously?

DOUGLAS: Yes.

AARON: Mandolin?

DOUGLAS: Yep. That too.

AARON: Fiddle?

DOUGLAS: Check.

AARON: I'll believe it when I see it. Dad, get him that banjo.

FRANK: We're eating.

AARON: Just do it. Jesus.

FRANK: We're having a meal here.

AARON: He's not eating!

FRANK: Son—

AARON: C'mon, just go get it. Let's hear him play.

(FRANK *looks at* AARON.)

AARON: You got something better to do?

FRANK: Yes.

AARON: What?

FRANK: Eat.

AARON: When's the last time you had this many people in your apartment?

FRANK: I don't know. I don't keep track of such things—

AARON: Never. You got yourself a party, Dad. You wanted me to have company. Let's celebrate.

FRANK: I used to have my book group—

AARON: That was a million years ago, I'm sure. And I've heard just about enough about that damn book group. Get that banjo over there—

DOUGLAS: I don't want to interrupt your meal.

HARRIET: (Please play something.)

DOUGLAS: What?

AARON: What did you say?

HARRIET: I said he's not interrupting.

AARON: Do you like him?

HARRIET: What?

AARON: This guy. What's his name again.

(Silence)

HARRIET: Douglas.

AARON: Are you in love with him?

HARRIET: No.

AARON: Then why are you whispering?

HARRIET: I don't know.

DOUGLAS: She's got a boyfriend. I've met him. Seth. Great guy.

FRANK: He was a very friendly person.

DOUGLAS: And very funny.

HARRIET: Actually. We're not together. Anymore.

DOUGLAS: You're kidding?

HARRIET: No.

DOUGLAS: Wow. You two looked so in love. What happened?

(*They all look at* HARRIET.)

HARRIET: I really don't want to get in to it now—

AARON: C'mon.

HARRIET: I don't want to bore you with my—

AARON: We're all ears.

HARRIET: I'd rather not.

AARON: C'mon. He cheat on you?

(*Silence*)

FRANK: Leave her alone.

AARON: He's an idiot. This *Seth*.

FRANK: Just eat your sandwich, son.

AARON: Then get the damn banjo, Dad.

FRANK: No.

AARON: Just do it. Live a little.

FRANK: We're eating.

AARON: Do it! God! We eat all the time, by ourselves, and now we have some half-way decent company in this rat hole! Let us enjoy it! Please! Celebrate!

(FRANK *looks at* AARON, *puts down his sandwich and goes to dig out a banjo.*)

(Silence)

HARRIET: Do you need some help, Frank?

FRANK: No. Thank you.

(DOUGLAS walks over to help FRANK.)

DOUGLAS: Are you sure?

FRANK: Yes. One moment please.
(He finally retrieves the banjo from it's precarious perch. He's a bit out of breath.)
It's a little dusty, I imagine.
(He hands it to DOUGLAS. Blowing on it)
I apologize for the dust.

DOUGLAS: No problem.

FRANK: New York is very dirty.

HARRIET: It really is.

(DOUGLAS looks it over.)

DOUGLAS: Wow, Frank. This is a gem. Fantastic.

FRANK: You think so?

DOUGLAS: Oh yeah.

FRANK: *(To AARON)* I told you. I know good things when I see them. I know good quality.

AARON: Okay, okay. Keep your pants on. This isn't *Antique Road Show*.

FRANK: What?

AARON: Never mind.

FRANK: I can see things that are special.

DOUGLAS: But, darn it, I'm afraid, it looks like two of the strings are broken.

AARON: Of course they are.

FRANK: Let me see.

(He looks it over.)

I fixed this once. But maybe it is too old now. I don't
know. The dust maybe.

AARON: Well, that's convenient for you, Douglas.

DOUGLAS: What?

AARON: Get that mandolin, Dad. I'm determined to
hear this New Yorker play Blue Grass.

FRANK: What do I look like to you, son? "Get this, get
that."

AARON: Who has two working legs here?

(Silence)

FRANK: That's no excuse.

AARON: Well, too bad. I'm using it.

FRANK: Get it yourself.

DOUGLAS: I'll, I'll get it. If you want—

FRANK: No. Please. Let him.

AARON: I can't.

FRANK: Try.

AARON: I can't.

FRANK: Go over there. You can reach it.
(Silence)
Try, Aaron.
(Silence)

AARON: Oh, it's so awful, isn't it, Dad, watching me
pity myself? It just makes your skin crawl, doesn't it.
(Silence)
How dare I, your son, allow myself the luxury of
suffering when you have known so much more than I
will ever know—

FRANK: Stop it—

AARON: LET ME SUFFER!

(Silence)

For once in my life, just allow me my own fucking pain! Let me be the center of attention! Let me suffer!

FRANK: Son—

AARON: Let me feel *my* pain, for one fucking minute, without comparing it to yours.

FRANK: I'm not. I don't—

AARON: You will always win! But let me have one minute for myself!

(Silence)

FRANK: Calm down.

(Silence)

AARON: Look at me? I'm useless.

FRANK: That's not true.

AARON: I used to walk seven miles every morning, and now I can't even feel my fucking legs. I could build houses. I had purpose. I could have sex. I could be productive. Now—

FRANK: You are still productive. You can go back to school, you can meet new people, you can try—

AARON: Will you just let me feel sorry for myself for one goddamn minute.

FRANK: And then what? What will it get you, this pity?
(Silence)
You still have your mind. Your mind is infinite—

AARON: I don't care!
(Silence)
Fuck my mind.

FRANK: Then you are worthless. You're right. And you have learned nothing from me.

AARON: See? See?!
(*He starts to laugh.*)
Oh my god.

FRANK: What?

AARON: It's incredible.

FRANK: What?

AARON: Everything comes back to you.
(*Silence*)
It's all about you.

FRANK: I am your father. I have important things to teach you. I have experiences—

AARON: Harriet, let me continue with the story of my father and his experiences.

FRANK: No—

HARRIET: I don't think we need to—

AARON: Douglas, I'm sorry you are coming in pretty far into it, and I'm sorry I don't feel like going back, suffice it to say, my dad survived the Holocaust, by tooth and nail, and landed in New York, okay?

FRANK: No.

AARON: Okay?

HARRIET: Aaron, I think this is making your father uncomfortable—

AARON: No, I want to finish. You need to know this. You too, Bowtie. This is important. My father, Frank Gromke, lands in New York, and meets my mother—

FRANK: That is enough—

AARON: Now, my mother, god rest her soul, is a catch. A real New York girl. Smart. Savy. And my father really wows her with his German accent and tale of escape and woe and triumph. She's never meet someone like him. The real bootstraps type.

FRANK: Stop it. Please—

HARRIET: Aaron—

AARON: Listen! Most the guys she knew came from pre-war families. And here's this handsome guy, with moxie, and grit, and a sadness in his eyes a hundred million years old, but such fight in his spirit, and well, he won her over. The orphan fairy tale—

FRANK: Why?

AARON: They get married. They have two boys. They build a life. Get a mortgage. Years pass. And guess what? She starts to hate him.

FRANK: Why are you doing this?

HARRIET: Aaron. Don't—

AARON: She starts to shrivel under his amazing story. She starts to feel the weight of carrying so much—

HARRIET: *Please.*

AARON: What?

HARRIET: Don't, don't hurt your father like this.

DOUGLAS: Yeah, we, we really don't need to go into all this now—

AARON: Why not?

HARRIET: It's upsetting.

AARON: It's his badge of honor. He is—

DOUGLAS: Why are you such an asshole?

AARON: What?

DOUGLAS: Excuse me for saying so, but you are really—

AARON: That's not very *enthusiastic* of you. Douglass.

DOUGLAS: Why are you so angry at your father?

AARON: Who said I was angry?

DOUGLAS: You seem—

AARON: I'm not angry.

DOUGLAS: What did he do to you?

(HARRIET *watches* DOUGLAS.)

DOUGLAS: He's one of the sweetest men in the neighborhood. Everyone knows him—

AARON: Indeed. He's a wonderful, wonderful man.

DOUGLAS: So what's your problem?
(*Silence*)
It's not his fault you're in that wheelchair, is it?
(*Silence*)
Is it? I really don't know. Did something happen—

HARRIET: Motorcycle accident.

DOUGLAS: Oh.

FRANK: Aaron, stop this—

AARON: You two love birds going to gang up on me now?

DOUGLAS: It just seems obvious.

AARON: Says the guy who wears a bowtie. (Obvious.) What seems obvious?

DOUGLAS: Well, again, if you don't mind me saying—

AARON: I do, very much, but—

DOUGLAS: You seem to be blaming your father for your misfortune.

AARON: You think so.

DOUGLAS: Yes.

AARON: Do they teach psychology at Juilliard?

DOUGLAS: Don't get me wrong, I yell at my father too sometimes, and blame him for stupid things just because, you know, he's around and he's my—

AARON: Your father has nothing on mine. Trust me.

FRANK: Aaron. Enough!

DOUGLAS: I didn't say he—

AARON: This man is David.

DOUGLAS: Then give him your respect. He's your father.

AARON: Fuck you.

FRANK: Enough!

AARON: Your father owns a stupid corner deli and you think you know anything about respect—

FRANK: Aaron, I am begging you—

AARON: Let me tell you something—

FRANK: I think this has been just about enough for our guests. I'm very sorry. I'm sorry for my son—

AARON: Do you know what my mother said to me, Douglas? When I was angry at my father? "You can't be angry with him. It isn't fair." When I cried because I skinned my knee in the street, or cried because some kid teased me? She said, "Cry now, Aaron because when we get home, you're father won't want to see your tears. Don't ever let him see you this way."

FRANK: Aaron—

AARON: "We don't want to upset him. We don't to bring up any bad memories for your father. He has seen enough. Don't add to his burden with your tears, Aaron."

FRANK: I never asked her to say that. To do that to you. That wasn't true. You could have cried all you wanted. You could have—

AARON: I want to cry now, Dad, and you won't let me.
(Silence)
I want to cry and cry.

(Silence)

FRANK: You're a grown man.

AARON: I'm wearing diapers.
(Silence)
I am wearing fucking diapers, Dad.

FRANK: Oh son.

AARON: It's so fucking unfair.

FRANK: I know it is.

AARON: I want to cry and cry.

FRANK: Aaron. My boy. Please. I love you.

AARON: Who will want me now? Like this? Look at my legs. My dick. Worthless.

FRANK: My boy—

AARON: I'm not like you.

FRANK: Yes you are—

AARON: I'm not!

FRANK: You have your own gifts, Aaron. You have to believe in yourself. You have to believe in your mind. Your talents. Look at Itzak Perlman. He, he is—

AARON: He is a fucking prodigy!

FRANK: You have gifts too.

AARON: Oh please. Please. Stop—

FRANK: You can't give up. You are special. Special. You are my son—

AARON: I don't want to be special. I want to be normal. I want to walk down the street again.

FRANK: Son—

AARON: I'd even take being like stupid Douglas here.
(To DOUGLAS*)*
Although, you're so fucking normal, you've turned
weird.

DOUGLAS: What does that mean?

AARON: And Harriet. What I'd give to be able to sleep
with you. I mean it. Oh fuck me. Look at you. You're
beautiful. You're sexy. It is torture to sit here and look
at you and smell your perfume and know that Douglas
will get in your pants, not me. He will be the one—

HARRIET: No—

AARON: With that tie.

HARRIET: That's not true—

AARON: Insult to injury.

HARRIET: No—

AARON: I saw how you looked at him just now.

FRANK: Aaron.

HARRIET: No—

AARON: I saw you!

(Silence)

HARRIET: He just surprised me. That's all.
(Silence)
I was surprised.

*(*DOUGLAS *tries not to smile, happy. He looks at* HARRIET.
Adjust his tie. Clears his throat)

HARRIET: There will be other women, Aaron.

DOUGLAS: Of course—

HARRIET: You will meet women who love you. You
will—

AARON: You can leave now. Both of you. You're grossing me out.

FRANK: It's my house.

AARON: It's mine now too, isn't it, and I want them out. The celebration is over.

FRANK: Son—

AARON: Out!

FRANK: I'm sorry, Harriet and Douglas. I am very sorry for my son. I am very sorry.

AARON: Don't apologize for me. Again, it's about you?

FRANK: I didn't say that—

AARON: This my fucking fate.

FRANK: Nothing is your fate.

(AARON *begins to roll out of the room.*)

AARON: Nothing but you. Everywhere I turn, it is you. I don't exist.

(FRANK *stops* AARON.)

FRANK: Look at me, son.

(AARON *won't look up.*)

FRANK: Look at me!

(AARON *finally looks* FRANK *in the eye.*)

FRANK: You exist because I crawled out of hell to bring you here. I crawled! Do what you need to do to mourn your body now, son. Cry. Shout at me. Beat me with your fists. But do not for one minute tell me that you don't exist because of *who* I am. I would rather you died on that motorcycle than to stand here and watch you waste what's left of your life with this kind of self-pity.

AARON: I would rather have died on it too.

(FRANK *begins to slap* AARON*'s face but stops himself.*)

AARON: I told you, I'm not like you.

FRANK: You think it is easy? To be like me? You think it is easy?

AARON: No.

FRANK: *(Tapping is own head)* Every day I wake and ask myself how I will live this new day. How? Can I do it? It is a battle in my mind, every morning. Can I do it? How? I have to work and work in my mind. Every day. I fight the shadows, the smells. Their screams. Every day I fight because I got to live. This is my job, to live. This is my duty. For everyone. I...

AARON: That is easier than living in your shadow, Dad.

FRANK: You think so?

AARON: Yes. Trust me.
(He exits into a bedroom.)

(Long silence)

HARRIET: Well. I think it's time—

DOUGLAS: I should get back to work. My dad is expecting me.

FRANK: Please send my apologizes. Let me give you some more tip. Let me find my wallet—

DOUGLAS: No. Please. It's alright.

FRANK: I am sorry.

HARRIET: We understand, Frank. No need to explain.

FRANK: He is a good boy. He is smart. He is very smart. He could have been...he has a great mind for math, you know.

HARRIET: Of course.

FRANK: A great mind for numbers. As a boy, he was best in his class.

DOUGLAS: I know he loves you very much.

(FRANK *looks at* DOUGLAS, *tries to smile.*)

FRANK: Yes.
(*Silence*)
We will be fine.
(*He pushes another smile.*)
We will find our way.

DOUGLAS: Sure.

HARRIET: Of course.

FRANK: Thank you for spending some time in my home. I appreciate the company. And Leonard here is the first dog I've ever had here, so thank you Leonard.
(*He leans down and picks up the dog. He hugs the dog in a deep long hug. And kisses the dog's nose*)

(*The dog licks* FRANK'*s face.*)

FRANK: Thank you.
(*He hugs the dog again.*)
Dog's are so simple. Their love.
(*He looks at the dog.*)
So complete and simple, your love.
(*He kisses the dog one more time.*)
Right, Leonard? Unconditional?
(*Speaks in Hebrew in the dog's ear*)
Elohim shebashamyim, ten li ko'ach
(*God in heaven give me strength*)
Ary she'bellibi, ten li ko'ach
(*Lion of my heart give me strength*)
Ten li ko'ach.
(*Give me strength*)
(*He finally puts the dog down.*)
Thank you for coming in for tea.

HARRIET: Thank you for the invitation. And please thank Aaron for buying dinner.

FRANK: I will.

HARRIET: That was very nice of him.

FRANK: Yes.

HARRIET: Frank—

FRANK: He will be fine. We will be fine. Yes.

(DOUGLAS *and* HARRIET *head for the door.*)

HARRIET: Have a good night, Frank. I'll see you soon.
(*She kisses his cheek.*)
And take off that scarf, will you? It's summer.

FRANK: Never.

HARRIET: Don't be a stranger.

FRANK: I will try.

(DOUGLAS *shakes* FRANK's *hand.*)

DOUGLAS: Bye Frank.

FRANK: Good-bye.

(DOUGLAS *pats* FRANK's *hand again before letting go.*)

(HARRIET *and* DOUGLAS *open the door.*)

(FRANK *stands among his things. He looks back toward the bedroom where* AARON *left.*)

(*He walks to his record player.*)

(*As* HARRIET *and* DOUGLAS *exit, and the door closes, music plays from the apartment, as the stage returns to the city sidewalk.*)

(*Outside the building*)

(*Evening*)

(HARRIET *and* DOUGLAS *stand stunned.*)

HARRIET: Well.

DOUGLAS: Yeah.
(*Silence*)
Do you want to…have dinner…sometime—

HARRIET: Yes.

DOUGLAS: Great. Wonderful.
(*Silence*)
I have to get back to work now.

HARRIET: Of course, of course. Go.

DOUGLAS: Come by in the morning?

HARRIET: I'll see you then.

DOUGLAS: Great.

(*DOUGLAS hugs HARRIET closely.*)

HARRIET: (I want to cry and cry.)

DOUGLAS: (Me too.)

(*DOUGLAS kisses HARRIET.*)

DOUGLAS: See you tomorrow.

HARRIET: Yes.

(*DOUGLAS lets HARRIET go.*)

DOUGLAS: Coffee's on me.
(*He exits.*)

(*HARRIET stands with LEONARD.*)

(*Lights shift back to day.*)

(*FRANK enters and looks up at the tree. Studying a bird.
[The exact same pose/place as the start of the play.]*)

(*HARRIET stands watching him.*)

(*She looks at the audience.*)

HARRIET: Frank is not forgotten at all.
(*Silence*)

Frank is remembered and remembered and
remembered.

(FRANK *remains staring up at the tree. He watches the bird
as it flies away.*)

(*Finally*)

HARRIET: Hi Frank.

FRANK: Hello Harriet. And little Leonard.

HARRIET: A little hot for that scarf.

FRANK: No. It's perfect.

HARRIET: I'm making one for Aaron.
(*Silence*)
I hope that's alright.

FRANK: Yes.
(*Silence*)
That's very kind of you.

(FRANK *and* HARRIET *stand looking at each other, as lights
fade.*)

END OF PLAY

www.ingramcontent.com/pod-product-compliance
Lightning Source LLC
Chambersburg PA
CBHW052223090426
42741CB00010B/2660